LONDON OUT OF SIGHT

exploring the city's secret green spaces

black dog
publishing

london uk

INTRODUCTION

London is not, on immediate impressions, a quiet city: it's the second largest in Europe when defined by the size of the population squeezed into the city boundaries, a dense network of taxi and bus clogged roads, day-long rush hours and near-consistent cacophony. But solace is abundant if you know where to find it.

London Out of Sight: exploring the city's secret green spaces looks to reveal a wealth of the capital's hidden bucolic treasures—as well as a few idiosyncratic aspects of the not-so-hidden ones. From austere, Gothic cemeteries to Botanical and Physic society hubs, grassroots community gardens, dense ancient woodland and working city farms through to expansive and rugged parks, tiny city squares and nature reserves, London has an incredible wealth of unexpected sites of green interest.

This exquisitely illustrated little tome is designed to help you find them. The book is arranged into five rough geographic sections: "Central", "North", "East", "South", and "West". We've assumed a little practical license with the placement of a few of the entries to allow for ease of use (thus, the easternmost stretches of the City proper are still within the "Central" chapter), along with relevant addresses, opening times and transport links to help you get a little more "lost" than perhaps you thought you could.

CENTRAL LONDON 12

NORTH LONDON   **44**

EAST LONDON

84

SOUTH LONDON 114

WEST LONDON

CENTRAL
LONDON

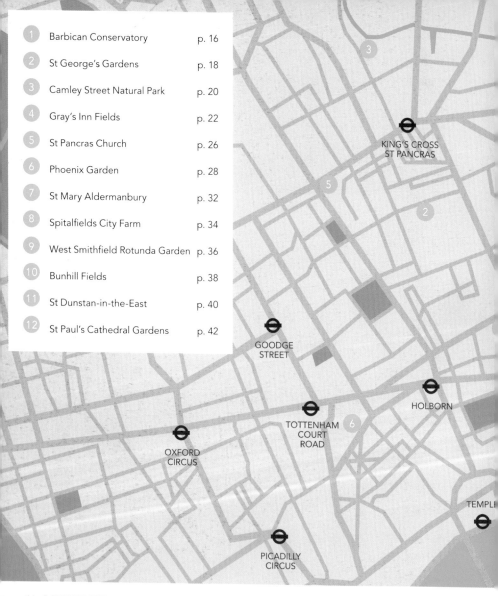

KING'S CROSS
ST PANCRAS

GOODGE
STREET

HOLBORN

TOTTENHAM
COURT
ROAD

OXFORD
CIRCUS

TEMPL

PICADILLY
CIRCUS

ANGEL

OLD STREET

SHOREDITCH
HIGH STREET

8

10

1

FARRINGDON

BARBICAN

9

ANCERY
ANE

MOORGATE

7

ST PAUL'S

12

MONUMENT

11

BARBICAN CONSERVATORY

Barbican Centre, Silk Street, EC2Y 8DS
Opening times variable—check www.barbican.org.uk
Stations: Barbican, Moorgate

The Barbican Centre—with its iconic brutalist exterior and extensive visual art, performance, music and film programme—is definitely no secret, though atop of its concrete structure sits the lesser-known glass-roofed conservatory. As a rule, the Londoners most likely to frequent the greenhouse are VIP types attending the exclusive parties and film premieres hosted within, but on Sundays and public holidays it's open to the rest of us, and for free.

The Conservatory—designed, like the rest of the Centre, by the eminent post-war modernist architects Peter Chamberlin, Geoffrey Powell and Christof Bon, though planted between 1980 and 1983—houses over 1,800 species of tropical and sub-tropical plants within its sprawling 3,675-square-metres of glass panelling. Specimens taken from locations as diverse as the bushlands of South Africa and the rainforests of Brazil include date palms, coffee bean trees and the endangered *Obetia ficifolia*, a kind of a pachycaul stinging nettle. In addition, there is also an Arid House attached to the building's east side, housing a large collection of cacti and succulents. An aviary within the Conservatory contributes to its vibrancy with an array of colourful birds including zebra finches, green singing finches, and Japanese quails, whilst a number of ponds within the space contain terrapins, ghost, grass and koi carp, roach, rudd and tench. The Conservatory also attracts a variety of outside wildlife.

Being so incongruously placed within the City's urban sprawl, the Conservatory is an alluringly lush oasis whatever the weather.

ST GEORGE'S GARDENS

Handel Street, WC1N 1NU
Opening times: 8am–9pm
Stations: Russell Square, King's Cross St Pancras

The meditatively peaceful St George's Gardens sits, hidden, between Bloomsbury and King's Cross. Designed as a burial grounds set away from the church it served, the gardens were set up in 1713 for two parishes, St George the Martyr at Queen Square and St George's of Bloomsbury. Where once a dividing wall split the area in two, there now lies chunks of broken headstones. St George's other gravestones have also been relocated and line the garden perimeters, though larger monuments have remained in authentic situ, dotted amongst the trees and foliage. The garden has maintained this appearance—aside from suffering some minor damage during the Second World War—since it was re-christened as a public space in 1890.

Prior to its current purpose—to provide Londoners with a little bit of greenery—St George's Gardens have seen a fair amount of gruesome history. It was the final burial place for dozens of Jacobites who were hung, drawn and quartered before being buried headless in nameless graves, and was also the cemetery from which the first recorded case of bodysnatching took place; in 1777 gravedigger John Holmes was found, with his assistant, carrying a sack that contained the body of Jane Sainsbury, who they had earlier buried in a shallow grave—a historic theft for which they were punished with a whipping, from Kingsgate Street to Seven Dials.

Despite the more macabre moments punctuating its history, the Gardens today maintain a quietly welcoming presence between the busy Brunswick Centre and Russell Square to the west, and Gray's Inn Road to the east.

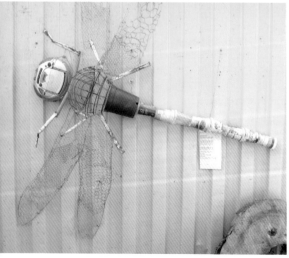

CAMLEY STREET NATURAL PARK

12 Camley Street, N1C 4PW
Opening times: 10am–5pm
Station: King's Cross St Pancras

Camley Street Natural Park is a two-acre green haven 'urban fringe' in the hotbed of redevelopment that is King's Cross Central, the area north of St Pancras and west of Caledonian Road. Running in a northern strip between Camley Street and the Regent's Canal—next to St Pancras Lock and adjoining the St Pancras Basin—the site is a tranquil collection of wooded paths and mixed woodlands, replete with a variety of ponds and a wooden cabin for a visitors' centre. The site provides an invaluable environment for myriad species of birds, amphibians, insects, butterflies, and aquatic and plant life.

Created from a disused coal yard in 1984 and placed under the guidance of the London Wildlife Trust, the subsequent work undertaken at Camley Street has gained the reserve international acclaim and attracted a wealth of public visitors, school groups and Trust volunteers.

The separate habitats maintained within the Park include mixed woodland with scrub and hedgerows; separate coppiced and deciduous woodlands; an area of marshland with red beads; a summer flowering meadow; and dipping and rainwater ponds, the water level of one of which is connected to and dependent on that of the adjacent canal.

GRAY'S INN FIELDS

High Holborn, City end
Opening times: Monday–Friday 12–2.30pm
Stations: Chancery Lane, Holborn

Surrounded by the barristers' chambers and offices of the Honourable Society of Gray's Inn—one of the four majors Inns of Court in the city—these Grade II* listed walled gardens, or Walks, provide a peaceful lunchtime respite from the bustle of the Theobalds and Gray's Inn Roads.

The landscaped gardens were originally designed by then-Treasurer Sir Francis Bacon in 1606, though the layout has changed since the eighteenth century. Previously, the Walks were known as Green Court and were open public lands. In 1587, the Society Pension approved the construction of a wall to render the gardens private, and by 1621—after myriad improvements initiated by Bacon—the Walks were considered to be "... the pleasantest place about London and that there you have the choicest society" by the Anglo-Welsh historian James Howell.

As the planting of trees and gardening of the area became conscientiously regimented throughout the 1600s, the Walks became a place of fashion. Samuel Pepys particularly noted the "many beauties" frequenting its avenues at this time; that is, before women and children were unceremoniously banned from the grounds in the 1700s (a rule not withheld today).

The key feature of the gardens is the broad gravelled promenade between an avenue of young red oaks and mature London plane trees that runs north from the gates at Field Court to a broad raised terrace, a feature leftover from Bacon's layout and now replete with a set of stone steps. Fauna throughout the walks include shrubberies, herbaceous borders and Indian bean trees grown from slips provided by Sir Walter Raleigh and subsequently planted by Bacon.

Gray's Inn Gardens
NOTICE

By permission of the Masters of the Bench the gardens are open to adult members of the public from Monday to Friday inclusive between 12noon and 2.30pm.

Members of the public using the Gardens do so entirely at their own risk.

Dogs are not allowed in the Gardens.

Cycling is prohibited.

The Head Porter has orders to remove any person causing or constituting a nuisance.

Master of the Walks

ST PANCRAS CHURCH

Euston Road, NW1 2BA
Opening times: 7am–dusk
Station: Euston

St Pancras Church, now nearly 200 years old, continues to exist as a functioning place of worship. Its key facet though—the extensive crypt hidden underneath it—is no longer a functioning burial complex, but now re-appropriated as a multi-use gallery and exhibition space. The dark, damp cellar is made up of a series of vaulted chambers, dimly lit with the occasional highlighting of an original burial plaque or a stack of grave markers laid up against one of the bare brick walls.

The church's exterior architecture is equally striking, particularly Charles Rossi's ornately sculpted Greek caryatids resplendent on the Euston Road side of the building. In addition, the Ancient aesthetic is further exemplified in elements included to imitate the original architecture of the Acropolis, such as the octagonal bell tower. On the south side of the church is a small, neat garden lawn, a quietly bucolic green space set in stark juxtaposition to the manic bustle of the Woburn Place/Euston Road crossroads. A point of interest here is Emily Young's elegant, melancholy sculpture of *Archangel Michael—The Protector*, installed in 2004 and inscribed in the memory of the victims of the 7 July bombings:

"In memory of the victims of the 7th July 2005 bombings and all victims of violence. 'I will lift up my eyes unto the hills' Psalm 1."

PHOENIX GARDEN

21 Stacey Street, WC2H 8DG
Opening times: 8.30am–dusk
Stations: Tottenham Court Road, Covent Garden

The Phoenix Garden, situated in a quiet spot north of Shaftesbury Avenue and east of Charing Cross, is the last of the seven Covent Garden Community Gardens. All of these—originally created by the Covent Garden Open Spaces Association, and which included Japanese, Chess, Italian and Water gardens—were built on vacant lots previously damaged during the Second World War. The Phoenix Garden's plot was for years put to unimaginative use as a car park, but in 1984 the area was revived and redeveloped as the beautiful, award-winning community space you see today.

A thin layer of poor soil covering a mound of Second World War rubble does not necessarily make for a biologically nourishing environment for an inner-city park, but the creators of the Phoenix Garden selectively chose plants suited to receiving little attention and poor growing conditions, whilst maintaining a broad enough variety as to ensure that the garden is visually interesting throughout the year. A by-product of this is the diverse range of habitats found within the Garden, which features an extensive assortment of wildlife, including several species of bees, butterflies and birds such as wrens, robins, blackbirds, woodpeckers and kestrels, as well as the only frogs in London's West End (allegedly).

ST MARY ALDERMANBURY

Aldermanbury, EC2
Opening times: 8am–7pm
Stations: St Paul's, Moorgate

Within London's extensive collection of historic churches, St Mary Aldermanbury has had a particularly interesting life. It was first recorded as a place of worship in 1181, but this original iteration was destroyed by the Great Fire of London in 1666. Rebuilt by Christopher Wren on the same site in Portland stone, it was decimated for a second time by the Blitz of 1940, with those stones that remained being transported in the mid-1960s to Fulton, Missouri and rebuilt within the grounds of the town's college in memoriam to Winston Churchill.

The original London site was taken over by the City of London Council and laid out as a green public space in 1970. As well as the remnants of St Mary's Medieval ruins, the leafy gardens house a monument to John Heminge and Henry Condell, topped with a bust of William Shakespeare in commemoration of their publication of the original folio of his plays and their artistic partnership with him at the Globe Theatre. The space is a Site of Local Importance for Nature Conservation, and a protected environment for wildlife, such as bullfinches, woodpigeons, house sparrows and blue tits, as well as myriad forms of insect life. The fauna chosen for planting in the Gardens—from herbaceous borders and *buddleia globosa*, as well as the naturally rampant ferns—reflects the considered intentions of maximising this.

SPITALFIELDS CITY FARM

Buxton Street, E1 5AR
Opening times: Tuesday–Sunday 10am–4.30pm
Station: Bethnal Green

Founded in 1978, Spitalfields City Farm is a volunteer-run charity located in London's Tower Hamlets borough, and the closest farm to the City's square mile. Though the Spitalfields area itself—not least the expansive covered marketplace—is these days a gentrified and bustling cosmopolitan hub, the farm is committed to the benefit of the wider local community, and seeks to help alleviate the stresses of the area's economic difficulties through urban agriculture.

1.3 acres of land provide space for animals and vegetable cultivation. The farm takes care of ducks, geese, sheep, ponies, pigs, ferrets and more; the two 'stars of the show' ostensibly being Bayleaf the donkey and Bentley the goat. The farm also contains an aviary that houses a wide array of exotic birds—a collection providing some extra colour and flare to the more muted rustic charms of the other residents.

The animals, as well as being a wholesome attraction, are used in staff programmes to increase awareness of animal welfare, provide demonstrations on how best to care for the species that are on show, and to give volunteers hands-on experience in urban agriculture. By offering so much to the community, be it entertainment or education, Spitalfields City Farm has helped to create an intimate link between the city and the country within a historically deprived area.

WEST SMITHFIELD ROTUNDA GARDEN

West Smithfield, EC17A 9BD
Opening times: dawn–dusk
Stations: St Paul's, Barbican, Farringdon

Sitting adjacent to the famous meat market, the West Smithfield Rotunda Garden has a suitably bloody history. Known as "Smooth Field" in the Middle Ages, it was infamous for its use as a public execution ground. Criminals, anarchists, heretics and martyrs—and William Wallace—have all met their fates on the site, which has existed in its current guise as a placid public space for over a century and a quarter. In 1305 the Scottish paladin was dragged by a horse and hung, drawn and quartered on the spot. Later, in 1381, the leader of the Peasants' Revolt, Wat Tyler, was hauled to the site from his bloodied respite at St Bartholomew's Church, still wounded by the Lord Mayor of London's attack. Earlier that day he had gathered his army in Smithfield after their march on London, but this enforced reunion with the grounds would coincide with his beheading.

In vast contrast, the Smithfield Rotunda now houses gardens that foster a wide range of plant life, providing a vibrant wild habitat in the area, with border planting and hedging providing shrub cover and sustenance to birdlife and an award winning insect hotel to inspire burgeoning apiarists and entomologists alike.

BUNHILL FIELDS

38 City Road, EC1Y 2BG
Opening times: 7.30am–dusk
Stations: Old Street, Moorgate

Bunhill Fields is a central London cemetery that dates back to the 1660s. As non-consecrated ground, the area was intended for—and particularly popular with—nonconformists of political or religious conviction, and up until its closure in 1853 it became the resting place for over 120,000 of them.

The grounds themselves are now Grade I listed and subsequently subject to fervent protection. 75 of the monuments within are themselves individually Grade II listed, including the obelisk to Daniel Defoe and the rather distinguished tomb of John Bunyan, Christian preacher and writer of *The Pilgrim's Progress*. Another grave of note is that of the poet and artist William Blake; his body is gone but his headstone remains, and though the memorial itself is surprisingly plain, members of the William Blake Society decorate it annually.

Many other graves at Bunhill invite intrigue for reasons other than simply the individuals they honour. For example, the huge marble chest commemorating one Dame Mary Page is—as a particularly macabre epitaph—inscribed with accounts of the illness that killed her in 1728, noting that her unfortunate tendency to water retention meant that "... in 67 months she was tapp'd 60 times, had taken away 240 gallons of water without ever repining at her case or ever fearing the operation".

Today, Bunhill Fields is divided into two sections, with the memorials secured behind a fence for preservation. Visitors can peer in, though not directly access them, and enjoy the shrub garden sitting adjacent.

NEAR BY LIE THE REMAINS OF
THE POET-PAINTER
WILLIAM BLAKE
1757 — 1827
AND OF HIS WIFE
CATHERINE SOPHIA
1762 — 1831

ST DUNSTAN-IN-THE-EAST

St Dunstan's Hill, EC3R 8DX
Opening times: 8am–7pm
Stations: Monument, Tower Hill

St Dunstan-in-the-East is one of the more subtly chimerical public gardens in London, and certainly one of the least conspicuous. Hidden down an alleyway of characteristic city steel and grey stone, the remains of a Medieval church resplendent with grass lawns, exotic climbing plants and lively flowers create an environment genuinely incongruous to its surroundings.

The church itself was first built around 1100, and, after suffering vast damage after the Great Fire of London in 1666, was mended by Sir Christopher Wren, who added a steeple and tower. More destruction was to come, and during the Blitz of 1941 it was bombed beyond repair. What remains now are its northern and southern walls, and the Wren steeple—all overcome by nature—complementing the alluring Gothic details.

Though St Dunstan may look like a forgotten ruin, the City of London Architects and Parks Departments meticulously designed the garden in 1971, subsequently winning a Landscape Heritage Award for their work in 1976. With green lawns, a fountain and benches dotted around the remains, it provides a welcome utopia for workers seeking a little solace from the relentless bustle and bluster closely adjacent: a haven for City refugees, if you will. At the weekend, however, it is particularly quiet and solitary.

ST PAUL'S CATHEDRAL GARDENS

St Paul's Churchyard, EC4M 8AD
Opening times: 6am–8pm
Station: St Paul's

The St Paul's Cathedral we recognise today is in fact the fifth incarnation of the structure to stand on the site, with Christopher Wren's iconic edifice being approved upon its third design proposal in 1675, with work finally being completed in 1712. A marble copy of the original statue of Queen Anne built to commemorate the event remains on the site today. By the middle of the nineteenth century the precinct of St Paul's encompassed these five sites of former churchyards alongside the cathedral forecourt. A desire for an integrated public space within these grounds followed, with an elongated discourse on the subject beginning in 1874 and an eventual agreement with the Dean and Chapter being made in 1878. On the 22 September 1879 the Lord Mayor opened the gardens to the public. To the south of the nave, the remains of a derelict chapter house cloister can still be spotted amongst the current groups of London plane, gingko, maple, lime, ash, mulberry and eucalyptus trees, whilst the northern gardens carry the prestige of housing some of the oldest London plane trees in the city and the area's only giant fir. A splendid rose garden completes the circuit of foliage toward the south gate.

The Queen's Diamond Jubilee Garden—which includes 378-square-metres of lawn and over 3,000 herbaceous plants, amongst a further extensive range of plant and tree life— is the newest part of the site, opened in April 2012.

NORTH
LONDON

GOLDERS
GREEN

HAMPSTEAD

KILBURN

SWISS
COTTAGE

KILBURN
PARK

ST JOHN'S
WOOD

WILLESDEN
JUNCTION

HORNSEY

SOUTH
TOTTENHAM

9

CROUCH
END

HIGHGATE

6

MANOR
HOUSE

1

ARCHWAY

10

FINSBURY
PARK

7

STOKE
NEWINGTON

11

KENTISH
TOWN

HOLLOWAY
ROAD

12

DALSTON
KINGSLAND

HIGHBURY &
ISLINGTON

11

CAMDEN
TOWN

4

EUSTON

KING'S
CROSS

ANGEL

3

HIGHGATE CEMETERY

Swain's Lane, N6 6PJ
Opening times: 11am–5pm
Station: Archway

Highgate Cemetery—designed by the architect Stephen Geary in conjunction with James Bunstone Bunning and David Ramsey, and consecrated in 1839—is a Grade I listed park. As with many other contemporary cemeteries, Highgate was constructed due to the early-nineteenth century population explosion. This partly accounts for its location on a hillside outside of the city's centre, though its height of 375 feet above sea level also offers a unique vista overlooking London.

The cemetery houses two chapels: one for the Church of England, and one for those referred to as 'dissenters', with both located in the same Tudor building. Alongside the abundant Gothic architecture are more overt examples of the Classical style, as well as structures with an Eastern influence; the Egyptian Avenue and Circle of Lebanon are structured in a way that matches the original contents of the Ashurst Estate, 17 acres of which were bought to build the cemetery upon.

The early success of Highgate allowed for expansion, and in 1856 the East Cemetery was opened (a tunnel connects it with the original westerly plot). Towards the end of the twentieth century, after having fallen into disrepair, the cemetery underwent something of a cultural renaissance, and preservation and restoration works were undertaken in order to maintain and recreate its individualistic beauty. The cemetery now houses a wealth of significant and aesthetically idiosyncratic graves and monuments, from the instantly recognisable bust of Karl Marx through Patrick Caulfield's angular headstone and the tribute-adorned but simple grave of sci-fi writer Douglas Adams.

HILL GARDEN AND PERGOLA

Inverforth Close, NW3 7EX
Opening times variable—check www.cityoflondon.gov.uk
Stations: Highgate, Golders Green

The Hill Garden was originally constructed as a part of the private gardens associated with Hill House in north London. Opened to the public in 1963, this hidden part of Hampstead Heath is now managed by the City of London Corporation.

The house itself was the 1807 home of the Quaker banking family Hoare, and its interesting history since includes several stints as a hospital, as well as a period at the hands of soap mogul Lord Leverhulme, who was responsible for the garden's most extensive re-landscaping. In order to connect Hill House's two remarkable gardens, and provide a location suitably idyllic for Leverhulme's social summer parties, construction of the raised pergola started in 1905 with the help of celebrated landscape architect Thomas Mawson. Raising the features of Hill House's gardens required the introduction of a mass of soil, something then readily available at the nearby site of the London Underground's Northern Line extension.

The pergola was extended twice in the early-twentieth century and, though it fades in comparison to its former splendour, it retains an indisputable beauty and ambience. Particularly striking when covered in climbing jasmine, wisteria and honeysuckle in the late spring, though spectacular at all times of the year, the 800 foot walk and the summer house at its point provide stunning spots from which to take in views of the city.

DUNCAN TERRACE GARDEN

Duncan Terrace, N1 8DD
Opening times: 8am–dusk
Station: Angel

Duncan Terrace is one link in a long chain of public spaces that make up the New River Walk. A green enclave surrounded by austere Georgian architecture and sitting on a length of filled-in canal, it has transformed into a meandering walkway, lined with beds of seasonally shifting perennials, bulbs and ferns. A timber boardwalk guides the inquisitive through a grove of trees that provide dappled shade on sunnier days, a perfect spot for respite from the much busier lawned area. A particular point of aesthetic interest to look out for is London Fieldworks' *Spontaneous City in the Tree of Heaven*—a tree part-covered in modernist bird boxes, and part of the duo's larger *Spontaneous City* project.

As well as being a prime standalone space, Duncan Terrace's connection to the New River Walk links it to one of London's more rambling pursuits. The walk was completed in 1613, and runs all the way from Hertfordshire to the New River Head in EC1. It is still possible to follow parts of the river route, as seen in the specific entry later in this chapter.

CULPEPER COMMUNITY GARDEN

35 Batchelor Sreet, N1 0EJ
Opening times: 10am–4pm
Station: Angel

Culpeper Community Garden—named after the area's renowned seventeenth century herbalist Nicholas Culpeper—is a small neighbourhood project in Islington. The little garden was a derelict dumping ground until 1982 when the local community, helped by a small grant from the council, began a renovation programme that aimed to transform it into a bucolic urban escape. One key intention was to provide an outdoor space for borough residents who didn't have their own, particularly the young people of the area, giving them the opportunity to work with nature. The garden continues to be maintained by the community that originally championed it, and today boasts vegetable plots and herb beds as well as other plants. The produce grown is sold locally as a part of the garden's sustainability programme, which also includes the promotion of composting and use of manure from nearby city farms.

Though proactive participation by the local community is integral to the upkeep and continuing life of Culpeper Community Garden, it is open to the public as well.

HAMPSTEAD HEATH

Accessible from Highgate Road (NW5),
Gordon House Road (NW5), East Heath Road (NW3)
Stations: Hampstead, Gospel Oak

Considering its location—just six kilometres from Trafalgar Square—Hampstead Heath is an astonishingly vast expanse. Covering 791 acres, the sprawling heath takes in ancient woodland, meadows and 30 ponds. Unsurprisingly perhaps, given this miscellany of habitat, it is an undoubted treasure for those seeking sight of wilder Britain: muntjac deer, foxes, rabbits and squirrels are common spectacles; bats, grass snakes, slow worms, frogs and newts require a more beady-eyed spotter; and over 180 bird species, including kingfishers and three breeds of woodpecker, frequent the area.

Fauna aside, the Heath also provides a spectacular panorama of London; take a walk to Parliament Hill for a particularly satisfying view of that iconic skyline which now features both The Gherkin and The Shard.

An abundance of recreational opportunities at the heath includes no less than four swimming locations; as well as a lido at Parliament Hill there are three swimming ponds—male, female and mixed. These open-air pools are enjoyable whether you're taking a summer dip or looking for somewhere to do your daily lengths, though only the sturdiest veterans brave them through the winter—perhaps surprisingly, the ponds are open every day of the year.

PARKLAND WALK

Finsbury Park to Muswell Hill via Highgate
Stations: Finsbury Park, Highgate

Tracing its way along the disused London and North Eastern Railway line, in the hills of London's Northern Heights, is a peaceful nature trail brimming with greenery and wildlife. Parkland Walk, as it's now known, follows the line in two sections; the southern stretch begins at Finsbury Park and runs through Crouch Hill to Highgate, the northern through Muswell Hill up to the railway's final destination, Alexandra Palace. The path is approximately four-and-a-half miles long and is appropriately, if not imaginatively, known as "London's Longest Nature Reserve".

Its nature reservation credentials are certainly well deserved. With over 200 species of wildflower, areas of endangered acidic grasslands, and an extensive variety of tree species, the walk is a slice of the countryside welcomed by cyclists and joggers as much as the hedgehogs, foxes and rare bees.

While it is fair to say that the environment has taken over since the railway's closure—patches of the path are encased by an arch of trees reaching overhead, and birdsong rings out loudly—colourful graffiti under the bridges, railway paraphernalia, Marilyn Collins' faintly unsettling Spriggan sculpture and even remaining abandoned train stations are instances of the human touch that intermittently remind you of its previous incarnation. But don't expect to venture along a track of inner-city detritus—Parkland Walk is wholly bucolic with only the slightest intrusion of urban life.

CLISSOLD PARK

Green Lanes, Stoke Newington, N16 9HJ
Opening times: 7.30am–dusk
Stations: Stoke Newington, Finsbury Park

Stoke Newington's Clissold Park was formally opened to the public in 1889. The 54-acre park was initially built for Jonathan Hoare, a prominent member of London's nascent abolitionist movement; following his death, ownership of the house and grounds were passed to the eponymous Reverend Augustus Clissold. Seven years after *his* death, the park was donated to the public.

The park was awarded a Green Flag in 2008, reflecting its sterling upkeep and variety of public facilities. Animal lovers will be kept busy by an aviary, butterfly dome and the park's deer enclosure. For those more sports-inclined, there are table tennis tables, tennis courts and a multi-use games area. Children are also catered for, with a large playground and a paddling pool for the 'hot' summer months. Clissold Park also hosts an organic market garden, run by the local Growing Communities collective.

It is also possible to factor a visit to Clissold Park as part of the wider Capital Ring walking route, a broader exploration of London's green spaces, taking in stretches of the New River, which skirts the park and provides clean drinking water to the city to this day.

KENWOOD HOUSE

Hampstead Lane, NW3 7JR
Opening times: 9am–6pm excluding public holidays
Station: Hampstead

Kenwood House, a vast eighteenth century stately home, is perched amongst stunning, preened gardens in a spot where a manor house has stood since the early 1600s. While the house itself is worth a visit—in particular the gallery, containing pieces by Vermeer, Rembrandt and Turner, amongst others—Kenwood's gardens are its main attraction.

In contrast to neighbouring Hampstead Heath—wild and organic in comparison—Kenwood's impeccable grounds remain ordered to their primary design; they were originally landscaped to produce a specific experience for the visitor, who, when walking along its snaking paths, come across a series of unexpected views and features.

These 112 acres are stately and laden with quintessential English charm. Attractions include a sizeable assortment of plants—some areas of the garden are even classified a "Site of Specific Scientific Interest" on account of their sessile oak and beech; the 'Sham Bridge', a strangely elaborate materialisation of the fashionable landscape paintings of the era which strikes the viewer as an exaggeration of eighteenth-century grandeur; and arguably the most enjoyable viewpoint—looking back across the grassland at the grand, imposing house itself.

QUEEN'S WOOD HIGHGATE

Between Muswell Hill, Highgate Village, Crouch End
and East Finchley
Opening times: 7.30am–dusk
Station: Highgate

Situated next to Highgate Wood and Muswell Hill Road, and one of three Local Nature Reserves in the Borough of Haringey, Queen's Wood is part of the Better Haringey Walking Trail. It is one of the borough's four ancient oak-hornbeam woodlands, rare areas of the original 'wildwood' which constituted much of the British Isles 5,000 years ago, and as such features an assortment of uncommon plant life that favours such 'primary woodland' ground.

Renamed in 1898 after Queen Victoria, the area was once known as Churchyard Bottom Woods, and the wood proper certainly retains the ethereal atmosphere of a place purported to have been the site of mass burial during the bubonic plague's devastating reign.

Somewhat chirpier, and certainly livelier, nowadays, Queen's Wood is loved by many nearby residents who contribute to its conservation and enjoy its extraordinary natural environment, the child and dog friendly community café, and the organic fruit, vegetable and flower garden.

ABNEY PARK CEMETERY

Stoke Newington High Street, N16 0LH
Opening times: 8am–5pm
Station: Stoke Newington

Abney Park Cemetery, situated just off Stoke Newington High Street, is one of the city's most iconic burial grounds and a vision of Victorian decorative excess. Built in the early-nineteenth century across the estates of Abney and Fleetwood House (the then home of poet and notable nonconformist, Dr Isaac Watts), the cemetery was a pioneer in multi-faith burial grounds. The first of its kind in Europe, the site reflects the autonomous beliefs of Lady Mary Abney and Dr Watts, the latter of whom is commemorated with an iconic statue at the heart of the cemetery.

With such values, Abney Park was a suitable final resting place with other nonconformists and dissenters, its occupants including Congregationalist, Baptist and Methodist ministers amongst others. Two notable residents include the Salvation Army's founding members, Catherine and William Booth.

The cemetery comprises a wealth of elaborate new Gothic gravestones and grand mausoleums. One interesting feature is its Egyptian Revival style entrance gate—the first of its kind in the capital and a cornerstone in the Egyptian revival scene.

Though Abney Park no longer accommodates burials, it remains a popular place for locals to commemorate their loved ones, with memorial trees, benches and locations for scattering ashes still offered. It also hosts arts and educational activities, and is a Local Nature Reserve; also originally conceived as an arboretum, the area maintains an impressive diversity of trees and a subsequently sizeable wildlife population.

NEW RIVER WALK PATH

From Stoke Newington to Islington
Stations: Highbury and Islington, Stoke Newington

The New River Walk is a three-mile inner-city stretch of riverside pathway, winding from Stoke Newington, through Canonbury and Essex Road, to Upper Street in Islington. This 'heritage' section is the most urban part of a longer stretch of 28 miles, which begins in the Hertfordshire countryside that surrounds the city.

The rather inaccurately titled 'New River' is neither of the things its name claims; the waterway is the remnant of a man-made aqueduct, constructed over 400 years ago to import clean water into the festering city. Since its redevelopment in the 1990s, the river has been an area for organic environmental growth; the water and its surrounding shrubbery together create a diverse, valuable habitat for city wildlife such as the ducks, coots and moorhens that can be spotted nesting in the area. Inevitably, being seasonally changeable, the area is stunning when the river freezes over during a cold winter, but positively swampy during the height of summer.

Evolution and diversion of the river over the years have ultimately made for a route comprising various elements; original portions are interspersed by tunnelled sections, straightened street sections (the grassed bank which runs up the centre of Petherton Road was also once an open section of the waterway) and larger open spaces— particularly charming is the basin area with scenic waterfall.

KING HENRY'S WALK GARDEN

11c King Henry's Walk, N1 4NX
Opening times: Saturdays 12pm–4pm, Wednesdays 10am–3pm
Station: Dalston Kingsland

King Henry's Walk Garden is an inspiration for those with green fingers and an eye for cultivation in the city. A showcase of biodiversity, the garden comprises a series of community vegetable allotments; an area of woodland (fondly known as "Docwra's Wood", presumably after Thomas Docwra & Son, a contractors who occupied the site until the 1920s) in which extraordinary efforts have been made to increase the variety of trees—37 new species, including oak, rowan, silver birch, whitebeam and hornbeam, were recently introduced to the area; and a staggering list of other plants, shrubs, flowers and herbs which includes no less than 18 varieties of fruit tree.

In addition to the fragrant abundance of plant life, there's a pond brimming with wildlife—over which a bridge has been built so visitors can get up close to the aquatically-inclined frogs and insects—and a series of beehives, maintained by garden volunteers.

King Henry's Walk Garden is also a charitable organisation that seeks to educate while it provides a green space for local residents, offering itself up as a 'garden classroom', in which several workshops and talks are conducted. As such, the garden is a valuable asset to the community as well as an organic oasis which continues the rich tradition of nurseries that have existed in the area since the late-nineteenth century.

EAST LONDON

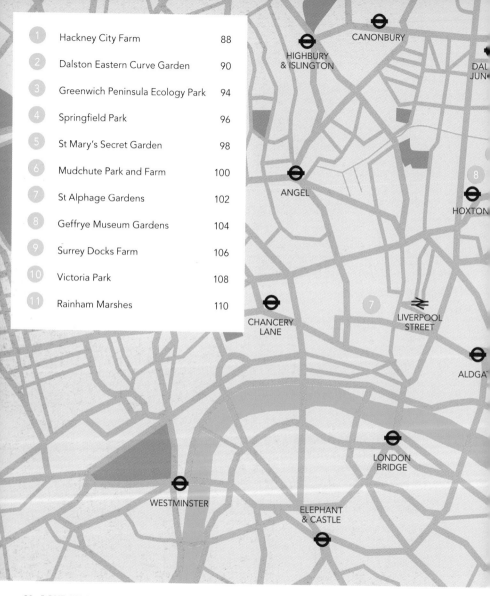

CANONBURY

HIGHBURY
& ISLINGTON

DAL
JUN

ANGEL

8

HOXTON

CHANCERY
LANE

7

LIVERPOOL
STREET

ALDGA

LONDON
BRIDGE

WESTMINSTER

ELEPHANT
& CASTLE

HOMERTON

HACKNEY WICK

STRATFORD

LONDON
FIELDS

10

BETHNAL
GREEN

MILE
END

BROMLEY-BY-
BOW

CANNING
TOWN

SHADWELL

9

CANARY
WHARF

NORTH
GREENWICH

11

3

MUDCHUTE

6

HACKNEY CITY FARM

1a Goldsmith's Row, E2 8QA
Opening times: Tuesday–Sunday 10am–4.30pm
Stations: Hoxton, Cambridge Heath, Bethnal Green

Officially established by locals in 1984, Hackney City Farm was built on a disused lorry park, thus reverting the site to its original use; at the beginning of the nineteenth century it was a hub of agricultural and commercial activity, with the land being used to rear animals and grow vegetables for the city. 80 years later it was providing another staple of the London diet, housing a brewery that supplied beer to the East End. From the 1940s onwards, the land was occupied by the Jeakins family's haulage company.

London's economy changed markedly over the years, and by the 1980s the land had ceased to house businesses. A nascent farm was in operation by 1982, and Hackney City Farm proper was in full flow just two years later. In a volte-face it moved away from a monetary focus and now seeks to reconnect Londoners with urban agriculture. It gives visitors a chance to interact with a varied array of animals, including donkeys, Golden Guernsey goats and (sizeable) Tamworth pigs, alongside some smaller residents like rabbits and guinea pigs. It operates in conjunction with a rural farm, and the livestock split their time between charismatically gritty Hackney and the more bucolic Kent countryside—a lifestyle many of us would sensibly be envious of.

Farm produce is available for purchase, and the site's Frizzante restaurant utilises food from the site; it was awarded *Time Out*'s "Best Family Restaurant" award in 2010, and is a perfect place to replenish any energy spent on a visit to the farm.

DALSTON EASTERN CURVE GARDEN

13 Dalston Lane, E8 3DF
Opening times: Saturdays and Sundays 11am–6pm
Stations: Dalston Junction, Dalston Kingsland

Situated on a former railway line, Dalston Eastern Curve Garden was constructed in 2010. The Eastern Curve line itself was closed in 1944, with the tracks being removed in 1965; after the line's closure the space fell by the wayside, but the intervention of the architectural collective Exyzt helped to regenerate the land. Exyzt emphasise creativity, play, and collective experiences in their work, and their influence is clear to see in the garden's design.

The space they have created is inherently multi-functional, with a wooden pavilion constructed to encourage communal gatherings. Florae have been selected on their likelihood to attract wildlife to the garden—hazel, birch, and butterfly bushes are prevalent—and there are raised beds for food cultivation. 'Contribution' and 'engagement' are the desired effects of its layout, and public events are regularly organised. The site will soon include the Pineapple Greenhouse, allowing for a diversification in what can be grown by the garden's green-fingered regulars, as well as affording the opportunity for children's workshops to take place in the winter.

The Garden site is currently under threat from a planned redevelopment of the Kingsland Shopping Centre; a great worry given that this kind of egalitarian community enterprise is a relative rarity in the midst of busy London life.

OUR CAFE SELLS:

Ice cold fresh
Lemonade
and refreshing
lemon verbena tea
and fresh mint tea

DALSTON
EASTERN
CURVE
GARDEN

GREENWICH PENINSULA ECOLOGY PARK

Thames Path, John Harrison Way, SE10 0QZ
Opening times: 10am–dusk
Station: North Greenwich

Greenwich Peninsula Ecology Park is situated on what was once a four-acre mixture of marshland and agricultural pasture. With the end of the nineteenth century, and the burgeoning industrialisation of the area, the natural habitat had begun to decline, having almost entirely disappeared half a century later. However, when industry began to finally fall away again during the twentieth century, the marshes started to naturally reclaim their territory. Today the area has been restored to the thriving natural environment it originally was.

The park now consists of two man-made lakes, both of which provide a fascinating display of local wildlife. Standard pond-life thrives within, with frogs, toads and newts in abundance, and the wider marshland is home to a great variety of birdlife. The park has its own hides that allow the keen ornithologist inconspicuous access to the winged displays—of special interest is the array of uncommon gulls: Caspian, yellow-legged and herring varieties have all made a home of Greenwich. In addition to the marshland, there is a sizable meadow that attracts its own array of bugs and insects.

Be it with snipes and rails in the winter, or with grebes and turns in the summer, Greenwich Peninsula Ecology Park allows Londoners to reconnect with the age-old marshlands that much of the city has since forgotten.

SPRINGFIELD PARK

Springfield, E5 9EF
Opening times: 10am–6pm
Station: Clapton

Tucked away in a corner of Upper Clapton, this large but little-known park receives a fraction of the recognition of Hackney's other sizeable green spaces. As it is, Springfield Park ostensibly exists as a private garden for local residents, but it holds much to appeal to the wider London public.

The parklands were originally the grounds of three private residences (Springfield House, otherwise known as the Whitehouse, is the sole remaining of these and now houses the park café) given over to potential housing development in the Victorian era. Private investors saved it when the house and land went up for sale in 1902, and three years later it was turned over to the London County Council. It received a Green Flag award—markers of the finest green spaces in the country—shortly after its 2008 centenary, celebrating 100 years of providing a quiet, impeccably nurtured solace for the urban public. The park factors a mixture of gardens, lakes, conservation areas, grassland, waterway towpaths, a Community Orchard and sections of the Lea Valley and Capital Ring walks.

ST MARY'S SECRET GARDEN

50 Pearson Street, E2 8EL
Opening times: Monday–Friday 9am–5pm
Station: Hoxton

St Mary's Secret Garden, named in homage to architect John Nash's lost church, is a regenerative project situated in Hackney. Local volunteers founded the garden in 1986 by clearing green space that had fallen into disrepair. Initially, under the banner of Thrive (a national charity promoting therapy through horticulture), it offered therapeutic support for people with disabilities and learning difficulties. In 2006 it was renamed St Mary's Secret Garden, and with this name change came a broadening of its remit. The garden now runs a multitude of community-focussed schemes, as well as continuing to strengthen its foundations in therapy.

The garden itself covers a little less than an acre, and offers a wide array of multisensory features. In addition to the woodland and wildlife meadow, there are working beehives for honeybees, herbaceous borders, and sensory herb gardens. All parts of St Mary's are fully accessible to wheelchair users. In addition, community service users, as well as local learners and volunteers, maintain the garden's beauty.

Aside from the Secret Garden's visual and olfactory appeal, its strong community ethic makes it a hidden delight among the bustle of the East End. The garden's commitment to biodiversity, organic growth and education makes for an inclusive and authentically idyllic space.

MUDCHUTE PARK AND FARM

Pier Street, E14 3HP
Opening times: 9am–5pm
Station: Crossharbour

Mudchute Park and Farm occupies a 32-acre site on the Isle of Dogs. The park is a local community scheme that seeks to benefit locals through a reconnection with nature and wildlife, and is the result of a 1974 public campaign against the development of land for a high-rise council estate. The Greater London Council backed down on their plans for the space, and it became a park for those in the locality instead. 1977 saw the formation of the Mudchute Association, who sought to maintain the land and ensure new alterations were carried out to benefit its recreational status.

The obvious main attraction here is the farm itself, which houses a broad collection of both domestic and non-native animals. Being one of the largest urban farms in Europe, Mudchute is able to offer the larger animals—namely pigs, sheep, goats, donkeys and, a little more exotically, South American llamas and alpacas—extensive space in which to graze and exercise. The farm's 'Pets Corner' is ideal for young children; they can interact with rabbits, guinea pigs, chipmunks, gerbils and some inquisitive ferrets in the frequent animal handling sessions. In addition to the residents proper, Mudchute Farm also houses a wide range of naturally occurring British wildlife and nature, and the Park's extensive fields offer a little taste of London's distant pastoral history.

ST ALPHAGE GARDENS

St Alphage Gardens, EC2Y
Station: Moorgate

Positioned precisely on the old wall of the City boundary, this area, alongside the Barbican, was one of London's most heavily bombed in the Second World War. The surrounds of the dilapidated tower of St Alphage Church, itself built upon the ruins of the fourteenth century priory of Elsing Spital, were selected as part of a post-war rejuvenation scheme in the mid-1950s as a joint directive of the Corporation of London and London County Council, with a portion of the scheme encompassing the facilitation of gardens and peaceful spaces within the design of a new business district. St Alphage Gardens are overlooked by a high section of the Roman city wall to their north side, with the wall's inset gate to the neighbouring Salters' Garden visible from within the grounds. Two lawns lined by benches, each ornamented with a single oak and magnolia tree respectively, are intersected from the adjoining roadway by a beech hedge. The garden leads onto a lower paved area to the west with further seating, shrubbery and foliage.

GEFFRYE MUSEUM GARDENS

Kingsland Road, E2 8EA
Opening hours: Tuesday–Sunday 10am–5pm
April–October
Station: Old Street

The Geffrye Museum is most famous for its displays of shifting period decor—exhibiting changes in the tastes, needs, and behaviours of middle-class Londoners from the 1600s onwards—though the Shoreditch site also features a series of outdoor garden rooms, displaying town garden fashions from the past four centuries, with their layouts and contents drawn from extensive research and analysis of drawings, maps, planting lists, diaries and literature from each period. These include the Jacobean Knot garden, an early seventeenth century garden with formal structure and raised beds, a recreational eighteenth century garden with stone paths and symmetrical plant beds, a nineteenth century garden with carpet bedding, shrubbery and greenhouse, and an Arts and Crafts inspired twentieth century garden, with a pergola for climbing roses encircling a pool.

Visiting both the museum and the garden rooms reveals the relationship between interior and exterior domestic fashions; changes in our taste in the decorative arts have, throughout the ages, influenced garden design, and in return nature has been a staple influence on the interior realm. The connection between the indoors and the outdoors is also shown in the award-winning herb garden, which contains 12 beds of over 170 herbs arranged by domestic use, from their culinary functions to their importance in the bathroom.

SURREY DOCKS FARM

Rotherhithe Street, SE16 5ET
Opening times: 10am–5pm
Stations: Surrey Quays, Rotherhithe, Canada Water

Situated in Rotherhithe, on the south bank of the Thames, Surrey Docks Farm is a functioning urban farm, and has been in existence since 1975. The farm initially stood on disused space in London's docks, before relocating to its current site in 1986.

Its 2.2 acres house an array of farmyard life: visitors can expect to see larger animals like Red Poll bulls and cows, Oxford Down and Ryeland sheep, a Shetland pony, Toggenburg and Anglo-Nubian goats, large white pigs and a Gloucestershire old spot boar. The farm also houses a number of birds for egg production; from Indian runner, crested and brown ducks, through African and Indian geese, bronze and white turkeys, and Rhode Island and brahma hens and cockerels. Children will be particularly enamoured with the rabbits, guinea pigs and ferrets available for handling sessions. The farm also has its own apiary, which is used to produce honey for sale in the shop. All of the site's animals also provide supplies for its lauded Frizzante Café—a kind of micro 'chain', with associated, and equally feted, establishments at Hackney and Mudchute farms.

On a more community-minded and benevolent bent, the farm offers several educational programmes for school children, as well as running projects for adults with learning disabilities.

VICTORIA PARK

Grove Road, Bow, E9 7DE
Opening times: 7am–dusk
Stations: Cambridge Heath, Hackney Wick, Mile End

Victoria Park—fondly known to some as "The People's Park"—is London's oldest park, created by way of a petition issued by Queen Victoria in 1840. At that time there was no open space in the East End; with a slum population of 400,000, this level of residential intimacy was a perfect breeding ground for contagious disease. Disconcerted by the abnormally high mortality rate of local residents, the establishment formulated a plan to increase recreational activity. 30,000 local residents subsequently signed the circulated petition, successfully demanding a royal park, the first to be specifically created for the public.

Victoria Park's 213 acres of open space covered what was previously poor quality land used for market gardens, grazing and gravel digging. It was flat, and had poor soil and no water, but its low-cost was attractive to planners. Designed by Sir James Pennethorne, it was an instant success with Londoners, who impatiently started using it before completion.

The park suffered heavy bombing during the Second World War, and some of the bridges to the lake islands were subsequently demolished. In addition, a violent storm in 1987 severely damaged parts of the site. However, in 2012 the park underwent a multimillion-pound regeneration, which included the installation of a new Chinese pagoda to replace the one damaged in the war, a number of newly built bridges to the islands, the creation of the Eastern Hub Building (housing a café, community room and park offices), and restorations of the Burdett Coutts Fountain and the Old English Gardens.

RAINHAM MARSHES

New Tank Hill Road, Purfleet, Essex, RM19 1SZ
Opening times: 9.30am–5pm, subject to change with seasons
Station: Purfleet

Rainham Marshes is an RSPB nature reserve situated alongside one of the easternmost stretches of the River Thames. Prior to its acquisition in 2000, the land had been off-limits to the public for a century; during those 100 years the site was used by the military as a firing range. After the acquisition, the RSPB re-imagined the site as a place in which life could flourish, and provided the public with access to the bucolic landscape.

Having a combination of both wetland and grasslands, Rainham Marshes is an ideal habitat for a diverse range of British nature. The change of seasons ensures that one can spot a vast number of migratory birds throughout the year, whilst the reserve also plays host to certain species all-year-round: with spring comes glimpses of stonechats, oystercatchers, reed buntings and marsh harriers; summer sees lapwings, whimbrels, black-tailed godwits, avocets and yellow wagtails; in autumn, merlins, peregrines, bearded tits, meadow pipets and barn owls; and dunlins, shelducks, golden plovers, little egrets and chiffchaffs are abundant in winter (amongst many others).

With the marsh tracks covering roughly two-and-a-half miles, it is no surprise that the Marshes are not simply a haven for ornithologists; water voles are a common sight, as are seals via the site's sea wall paths. Lastly, the reserve's amazing retro-futurist visitor centre is its natural hub; aesthetically idiosyncratic but thoughtfully designed so as to not impact visually on its surroundings.

SOUTH LONDON

SOUTHWARK

LONDON
BRIDGE

10

BERMONDSEY

1

ELEPHANT
& CASTLE

SURREY
QUAYS

9

13

2

4

OVAL

QUEEN'S ROAD
PECKHAM

N
CR
G

DENMARK
HILL

PECKHAM
RYE

NUNHEAD

8

CLAPHAM
NORTH

BRIXTON

3

NORTH-
DULWICH

HONOR OAK
PARK

6

12

WEST
DULWICH

FOREST HILL

11

5

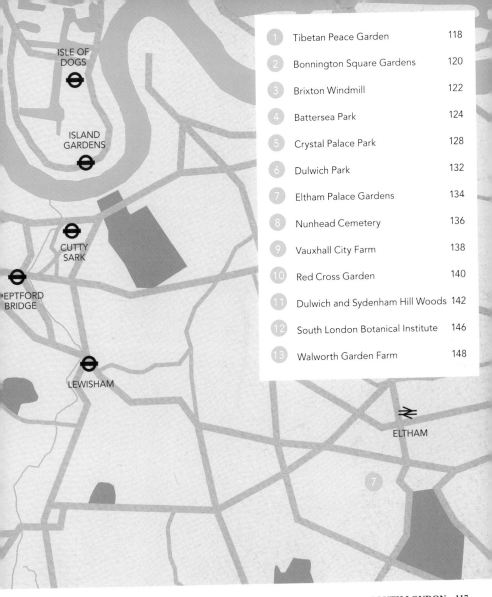

ISLE OF DOGS

ISLAND GARDENS

CUTTY SARK

EPTFORD BRIDGE

LEWISHAM

ELTHAM

7

TIBETAN PEACE GARDEN

Imperial War Museum, Lambeth Road, SE1 6HZ
Opening times: 10am–6pm
Station: Lambeth North

In a poignant juxtaposition, the intimate Buddhist Peace Garden lies serenely next to its imposing neighbour, the Imperial War Museum. Commissioned by the Tibet Foundation, the garden was built as a monument to the Tibetan people and a promotion of the Buddhist belief in non-violence, providing Londoners with a place to consider the benefits of peace next to a display of conflict's influence (its Tibetan name, *Samten Kyil*, means 'garden of contemplation').

Whether or not the visitor intends to learn about Buddhist values, the space provides a relaxing environment, with fragrant herbs, jasmine, honeysuckle and roses sitting alongside other Himalayan plants. The design of the garden does, however, fit in accordance with Buddhist philosophy. Arranged around the Noble Eightfold Path (a principal Buddhist guide for reaching righteousness) are several benches providing meditative spots for introspection. In addition, four modern sculptures representing the elements sit at the northern, southern, eastern and western entrances. A 'Language Pillar' displays a message from the Dalai Lama, who opened the garden in 1999, encouraging communication and consideration amongst all cultures and individuals alike, appropriately carved in Tibetan, English, Chinese and Hindi. These features come together around a circular centrepiece—an elaborately carved stone emblem of world peace, the Kalachakra Mandala.

The Kalachakra Mandala says a lot about the garden itself; like the central sculptural features of numerous gardens around the capital, its intricate beauty captures the attention of passers by and visitors, whilst also embodying a beautiful message. The Buddhist Peace Garden not only presents a pleasant and tranquil hidden space for the stressed Londoner, but also signifies a more meaningful need for contemplation.

BONNINGTON SQUARE GARDENS

Bonnington Square, SW8 1GA
Opening times: Saturdays and Sundays 10am–5pm
Station: Vauxhall

Bonnington Square Gardens form the central communal area, affectionately known as Vauxhall Pleasure Garden, of an area of co-operative housing tucked behind the high-rise flats of South Lambeth Road, and is today considered one of the finest community gardens in London.

Where once six houses occupied the land, a beautiful organic garden has taken over. Unlike other preened and manicured small London squares—though by no means less cared for—the gardens present an organic explosion of nature that has been collaboratively nurtured by a community for over 20 years.

After time as a failed open play space and an abandoned area of little value, locals—two of whom were garden designers—invested their time and effort to revive the space into a shared idyll. Using their imagination and ingenuity, many members of the community contributed, donating plants or other idiosyncratic features including an abandoned boat found on Brighton beach and a marble-cutting waterwheel centerpiece, sourced from a disused factory.

The garden itself is situated in the centre of Bonnington Square, where the railings, posts and benches have now too succumbed to the gardens' honeysuckle and climbing plant life. Reflecting this, the innovation of the square's reformers has spread throughout the local area and led to the introduction of more plant life on surrounding streets.

BRIXTON WINDMILL

West end of Blenheim Gardens, SW2 5EU
Opening times: 8.30am–6.30pm
Station: Brixton

The sole survivor of 12 windmills that once existed throughout Lambeth, Brixton Windmill is a restored, functioning, Grade II listed structure in the eponymous Windmill Gardens, just off Blenheim Gardens.

This idiosyncratic landmark has survived a long and varied career; built in 1816, the windmill was originally sail-driven (known as Ashby's Mill, it produced stoneground wholemeal flour) until 1864 when it was relegated to a glorified storage unit. The early-twentieth century saw it used once more, though this time powered by gas and steam, returning the industry to Brixton until miller Joshua-John Ashby died and it fell into sad dereliction.

Following a lengthy cycle of restoration and vandalism, the windmill was recently finally salvaged by English Heritage and the Friends of Windmill Gardens—its latest restoration revealed the area as it can be seen today. The renovated windmill is today the focal point of gardens where heritage barley and wheat are grown to be ground in the mill once more. Open throughout the summer, the mill and gardens host an array of events for children and adults alike, themed around the history of the site, cultural heritage, local history conservation and ethical food production.

BATTERSEA PARK

Albert Bridge Road, SW11 4NJ
Opening times: 8am–dusk
Station: Battersea Park

Once the setting for a duel between the Duke of Wellington and the Earl of Winchester in 1826—during which, it might be added, neither man aimed to hit his opponent—the riverside site of Battersea Park has had a long and varied history, although it has only officially been deemed a public park since 1846.

Home to a broad array of flora and fauna, and considered by some as an interesting arboretum in its own right due to the abundance of rare specimens, Battersea Park feels like a window into the countryside; a notion only strengthened by its lodges and rustic bridge, features more commonly seen in the grounds of manor houses than city parks. Along with various garden areas, there are a number of sculptures from notable artists such as Henry Moore and Barbara Hepworth waiting to be discovered by visitors, including one in commemoration of the animal victims of vivisection. Out of season, there is plenty to engage with indoors as well as out: the Pump House Gallery is a Grade II listed building, home to four floors of contemporary art.

CRYSTAL PALACE PARK

Thicket Road, SE19 2GA
Opening times: 7.30am–dusk
Station: Crystal Palace

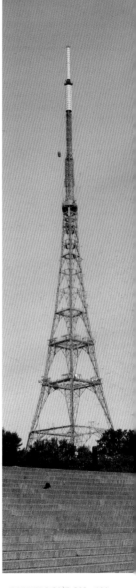

Arguably south London's grandest park, Crystal Palace Park was appropriately modelled in the 1850s to house a repositioned Crystal Palace, the ornate glass exhibition space designed for Prince Albert's 1854 Great Exhibition by Sir Joseph Paxton, of whom a celebratory effigy remains in the park. Though Paxton's seminal structure was devastated by a fire in 1936, the expansive park itself has more than enough points of interest to make it one of the city's most alluring green areas. Amongst its abundance of open space, a boating lake and a maze, features include the multi-use national sports centre at its core, an innovation of the 1960s.

Perhaps the biggest draws are the park's truly idiosyncratic sculptural elements. The landscaped lawns, woodland and lakes provide a comfortable habitat not only for the observable birds and wildlife, but also to 33 dinosaur sculptures installed in the park at the time of its public opening. Created in collaboration between Benjamin Waterhouse Hawkins, a natural history artist, sculptor and director of the fossil department for the then new Crystal Palace, and Richard Owen, founder of the Natural History Museum and pioneering palaeontologist, the dinosaur figures present an early visualisation of pre-historic creatures from very initial aesthetic comprehensions; charmingly naïve idiosyncrasies such as the rhinoceros horn inaccurately assigned to an Iguanodon, are explicitly intact.

DULWICH PARK

College Road, SE21 7BQ
Opening times: 7.30am–dusk
Stations: West Dulwich, North Dulwich

Dulwich Park is a 29-hectare green space between Dulwich Village and the top end of East Dulwich's bustling Lordship Lane, with Belair Park a little to the west past the wonderful Dulwich Picture Gallery at the Park's Old College Entrance, and Dulwich and Sydenham Hill Woods a short walk to the south.

The park itself is a bucolic mix extensive lawns, a large lake with wooden boardwalk, cascades and rivulets, copse-land, conservation areas, and jogging track, as well as further sports facilities including tennis courts, table tennis tables and outdoor gym equipment. Boating takes place on the lake in good weather, and recumbent bicycles can be hired for whizzing around the park's carriage drive. The park was once home to Barbara Hepworth's sculpture *Two Forms (Divided Circle)*—shamefully stolen by scrap metal thieves in 2011—and the increasingly ubiquitous street artist Stik is responsible for the Bowling Green Clubhouse mural, in addition to an extensive 2013 commission from the Picture Gallery.

Dulwich is a particularly pleasant example of Southwark's city parks, sedate and serene in the early mornings, evenings and in the low seasons, and buzzing with activity and community festivals on weekends and in the summer.

ELTHAM PALACE GARDENS

Court Yard, SE9 5QE
Opening times: 10am–5pm
Stations: Eltham, Mottingham

Eltham Palace is one of London's few remaining Medieval palaces, adjacent to which sits a 1930s house commissioned by its then proprietors, the stylish couple and enthusiastic horticulturalists Stephen and Virginia Courtauld. In addition to a rich monarchical history—having been home to both Edward II and later Henry VIII—the palace and its land have been previously leased to farming tenants and were, for almost half of the nineteenth century, occupied by army educational units. This multifarious combination of Medieval grounds, an extensive, varied history and the Courtaulds' modern effect has led to gardens formed by a patchwork of influences.

Spread over 19 acres, the gardens feature beautiful weeping willow trees alongside the original Medieval walls and bridge that once crossed the enclosing moat, which, no longer being necessary for defending the manor, now houses a series of garden rooms that were laid out during the Courtaulds' occupation. Visitors can advance through a fragrant sunken rose and lavender garden, rock garden, woodland garden and spring bulb meadow, all maintained today by English Heritage. The variety of plants found at Eltham Palace is extensive and represents not only those typically popular at home—though several areas present a quintessential English garden—but also some rather more exotic species, such as the Japanese Bitter Orange.

NUNHEAD CEMETERY

Linden Grove, SE15 3LP
Opening times: 8.30–dusk, subject to change with seasons
Station: Nunhead

Nunhead Cemetery is one of the lesser-known members of the 'Magnificent Seven', a collection of elaborate cemeteries developed on the outskirts of London to overcome the morbid ramifications of rapid population expansion in the late-eighteenth century. Opened in 1840 as All Saints' Cemetery, the graveyard covers 52 acres, a network of gravel lanes both circumventing and weaving past burial sites of varying extravagance, from carved angel sculptures and ornate headstones, to elaborate tombs and crypts.

Consistent with the archetypal vision in Victorian graveyard design, fine Gothic architectural details are abundant around Nunhead Cemetery, conspicuous in the ornately symbolic main gates which feature such icons of death as an ominous empty hourglass. The eerie feel of the cemetery does not solely result from such affectations, but also from the overgrown greenery engulfing it. After the Second World War it fell into neglected disrepair and after a lengthy and intensive period of restoration, was reopened in May 2001, by which time 50 memorials had been restored, along with Thomas Little's Anglican Chapel.

The site is now a partially designated nature reserve, and thus much of the fauna left to flourish in the years of closure is now protected. As well as providing an environment for a wealth of resident wildlife, it also affords a particularly haunting atmosphere and quietly archaic aura.

VAUXHALL CITY FARM

165 Tyers Street, SE11 5HS
Opening times: Wednesday–Sunday 10.30am–4pm
Station: Vauxhall

A short walk from the traffic-packed Vauxhall tube and railway stations exists a little slice of rural Britain. Over its modest one-and-a-half acre plot, Vauxhall City Farm offers a surprisingly extensive insight into the authentic day-to-day of farm life. An award-winning collection of animals includes pigs, goats, alpacas, ferrets, guinea pigs and rare-breed sheep. In addition, several ponies and horses form the basis of a small riding school, which offers both lessons and riding therapy sessions in the farm paddock. Visitors are also able to learn about grooming the horses and can take part in hands-on animal care.

The farm—which is free to visit—boasts an allotment, a duck pond and an ecology garden featuring its own bog, wormery and stag beetle nursery. As well as hosting various educational projects and a horticultural therapy group, the farm forms a hub for the Vauxhall City Farm Spinners—a society of textile enthusiasts and craftsmen who continue to employ traditional means of spinning the sheep and alpaca wool and dying it using the natural dyes available from plants grown on site.

RED CROSS GARDEN

Red Cross Way, SE1 1HA
Opening times: Saturdays and Sundays 10am–5pm
Stations: London Bridge, Borough

The Red Cross Garden is located between Borough High Street and Southwark Bridge Road, not far from the olfactory hotbed of Borough Market on the Thames' South Bank. Comparatively quiet, the garden features a number of places to recline and relax, flowerbeds, lawns and a charming pond with fountain and bridge. Overlooked by a quaint row of Tudor-style cottages, from certain perspectives the square could be mistaken for an archaic rural hamlet. As such the garden provides a pleasant respite space in the midst of the city for urban and community workers alike, a vocation in keeping with its original role. The Red Cross Garden was conceived in 1887 by Octavia Hill, philanthropist and co-founder of the National Trust, who, in establishing a local community housing scheme, insisted on the inclusion of an 'outdoor sitting room', a place where local residents could relax and urban children could experience nature.

With that ethos in mind, the garden remains a great success. It was awarded a "gold award" in Southwark in Bloom 2010, a Green Flag Community Award in 2011–2012 and a rank of "outstanding" in Your Neighbourhood Britain in Bloom 2012.

Such commendations, along with the considerable volunteer support received by the Red Cross Garden and the varied events held there regularly, suggest that more than a century after its inception the park remains a much loved part of the area, true to Octavia Hill's original vision.

DULWICH AND SYDENHAM HILL WOODS

Between College Road, Sydenham Hill and Lordship Lane
Stations: Forest Hill, Sydenham Hill

The dense, converging woodlands of Dulwich and Sydenham Hill provide one of the more quietly immersive natural environments in London. Together with the oak-lined avenue of Cox's Walk, they constitute the largest remaining tract of the Great North Wood—a large swathe of oak and hornbeam forest that stretched along the ridge of land between Deptford, Selhurst and Streatham.

The expansive woods are a dense mixture of ancient and modern woodland, Victorian garden relict trees—in this case a monkey puzzle and a cedar of Lebanon—and a hub for a diverse range of wildlife (keep your eyes open for stag beetles, bats and woodpeckers in particular).

Points of interest abound throughout the area: a crumbling Victorian folly of an abbey provides an atmospheric distraction to the circular walk through Sydenham Woods; the sinister entrance to the impenetrable Paxton Tunnel, an old underground train track to Crystal Palace now inhabited by bats and inspiration to numerous urban legends (such as the gruesome tale of a commuter train and its passengers forever encased after a tunnel collapse); and a footbridge at the intersection of Cox's Walk and the woods proper, sitting over the old track bed, and from which—in its former wood and brick guise— Pisarro painted his meditative view towards Lordship Lane station, the aspect now overgrown.

SOUTH LONDON BOTANICAL INSTITUTE

323 Norwood Road, SE24 9AQ
Opening times: Thursdays 10am–4pm, or by appointment
Station: Tulse Hill

The South London Botanical Institute has endeavoured to educate and interest ordinary Londoners in botany for over 100 years. Alongside a substantial library of botanical reference books, journals and monographs—housing tomes on anything and everything on a spectrum from ecology and habitats, to fungi and botanical painting—the Institute is home to a herbarium (a catalogue of dried, pressed and mounted plant specimens originating from all across Europe and the UK) which is of both general interest and an academic aid to Institute members, who can use the archive in the identification of their own dried discoveries.

The highlight of the Institute is found through a small conservatory in which species favouring warmer temperatures and the carnivorous collection are kept: the smallest botanical garden in London (measuring a miniature 24 x 16 metres) which, incongruously to its title, holds an extensive collection. Over 500 plants, from native specimens to exotic flora, are showcased in a series of themed flowerbeds that include a medicinal garden; 'Gerard's border' (of the eponymous John Gerard, creator of an extensive 1596 list of herbal plants); and a border representing species from the Southern Hemisphere. Grouped with a pond used for cultivation of a variety of wetland plants (as well as livelier frogs and newts), the densely populated Institute provides a fascinating world tour.

WALWORTH GARDEN FARM

Manor Place, SE17 3BN
Opening times: Monday–Friday 9am–4.30pm,
Saturday 10am–2pm
Station: Kennington

Walworth Garden Farm is a working farm and community-training centre that has been going strong since its inception in 1987. As well as sustaining vegetable plots, flowerbeds, a colony of resident bees and an array of natural wildlife, the established project promotes small-scale community development with its myriad activities and opportunities for those wishing to participate.

The farm's wildlife club, environmental education sessions in surrounding schools and School Orchard Project (planting fruit bearing trees in playgrounds throughout the city) aim to spark ecosystem interest in Southwark's children. A horticultural therapy programme, Greenfingers, engages adults with learning difficulties or mental heath problems in gardening for therapeutic purposes, and gardening qualifications are available via a work scheme for 16–25 year olds. The introductory courses provide skills and practical experience necessary for pursuing a career in horticulture, as well as support for key literacy and numeracy skills, and advice on applying for jobs, all of which has gained the training centre an excellent track record in the number of young people it has helped to advance to full-time employment or further training.

All of these elements come together in demonstration of Walworth Garden Farm's mission: to increase local awareness of ecological issues and sustainable processes while promoting community inclusion. Its successes in these endeavours have been recognised in several awards, including four Green Flag Community Awards and a "gold" in the Best Community Area Award for Southwark in Bloom.

WEST LONDON

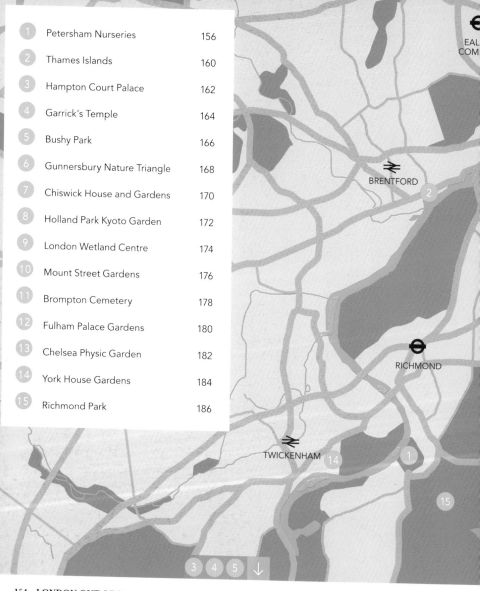

EAL
COM

BRENTFORD

RICHMOND

TWICKENHAM

QUEENSWAY

13

HOLLAND
PARK

8

CHISWICK
PARK

10

SOUTH
KENSINGTON

7

13

CHISWICK

9

11

FULHAM
BROADWAY

BARNES

12

PUTNEY
BRIDGE

EAST
PUTNEY

PETERSHAM NURSERIES

Petersham Road, Richmond, TW10 7AG
Opening times variable—check www.petershamnurseries.com
Station: St Margarets, Richmond

Petersham Nurseries, the internationally acclaimed garden centre and epicurean's dream, is a green haven within a borough resplendent in them. With views of the Thames, Petersham Meadows and Richmond Park, the gardens of Petersham House in which the Nurseries are set make for an excellent arena for walking. As is to be expected, the garden is replete with a variety of colourful flowers including romneya, macleaya, rheum, eupatorium, irises and oriental poppies, all of which are available for purchase at the nurseries.

After perusing the plants, it's well worth cocking a snook at the Nurseries' two eateries. Whilst the informal Teahouse provides an Italian-inspired menu, as well as a selection of whole-leaf teas, filter coffee and daily homemade cakes, it is the better known Petersham Nurseries Café which has drawn a wealth of critical acclaim. Opened in 2004, the Café is housed in the charismatic settings of one of Petersham Nurseries' greenhouses, where climbing plants scale the structure's glass walls and potted plants adorn each of the rustic tables. Since opening, its chefs have maintained a reputation for exemplary food produced with high-quality ingredients, thoughtful sourcing and an ethos of sustainability—the Café also uses edible flowers and herbs grown in their own Walled Kitchen Garden.

THAMES ISLANDS

Viewable from Thames riverside
Stations: Kew Bridge (Oliver's Island), Chiswick (Chiswick Eyot),
Isleworth (Isleworth Ait)

The extensive River Thames contains over 80 small islands—colloquially known as "aits" or "eyots"—which provide a subtle wealth of fascinating historical trivia, as well as valuable and inaccessible homes for local wildlife. We've picked a few of interest around the greater west London area.

Near Kew Bridge, and viewable from the charming riverside promenade of Strand on the Green is Oliver's Island. Originally known as "Strand Ayt", it attained its current moniker in the eighteenth century due to an apocryphal story, which suggested that Cromwell based a secret headquarters on the island during the English Civil War, access to which he gained via a secret tunnel. Aside from this hazy etymology, Oliver's Island offers a zone of contemplative charm. Herons, as is the case with many of the Thames Islands, are a large presence, as are cormorants and Canada geese.

Close by is Chiswick Eyot, a small island with a history stretching back to the Industrial Revolution. During low tide one can walk onto the island for a peaceful stroll between willows and reed beds.

Further west is Isleworth Ait—home to a surprisingly diverse number of creatures including the uncommon and intriguingly named two-lipped door snail and the German hair snail, bustling tree-creepers, kingfishers and an array of rare beetle species—accessible only on specified open days, but with local pubs offering excellent views of its waterfront.

HAMPTON COURT PALACE

East Molesey, Surrey, KT8 9AU
Opening times: 7am–6pm
Station: Hampton Court

Amid the grand Home Park, with its 700 acres of parkland, ponds, waterways and grand, tree-lined avenues stands Hampton Court Palace. The favoured home of Henry VIII—and prison to the ill-fated Charles I—the palace blends Tudor architecture with later seventeenth century additions by Sir Christopher Wren. From its very beginning it was designed to be the most impressive palace in England, an accolade that it arguably still holds.

The gardens that surround the palace combine stunning design with an impressive array of distinctively landscaped areas and individual plants. These include the famous yew-tree maze, comprising half a mile of paths; the iconic Knot and Privy gardens, the latter based on a design dating from 1702, symmetrically laid out and incorporating original marble sculptures and plant varieties; Rose and Pond gardens; the seasonally-changeable Lower Orangery Exotics Garden; and the Great Vine, planted by the esteemed designer Lancelot 'Capability' Brown and now boasting a base circumference of four metres, with a yield of around 600 pounds of grapes a season (available in the Palace shop!).

Hampton Court also plays host to two annual celebrations: the RHS Hampton Court Palace Flower show—a less crowded and for many, more favourable alternative to the Chelsea Flower Show—and the Hampton Court and Dittons regatta, a traditional boating event, featuring skiff and punt racing, which has been held since the late-nineteenth century.

GARRICK'S TEMPLE

Hampton Court Road, TW12 2EN
Opening times: dawn–dusk
Station: Hampton Court

Garrick's Temple was created in dedication to England's great literary icon, William Shakespeare. Built in 1756 by David Garrick, a famous manager and actor in his own right, the Classical octagonal shape construction is situated amidst a pleasure garden on the northern bank of the River Thames. Garrick's Lawn, which surrounds the shrine, was (supposedly) designed by the esteemed landscape architect Lancelot 'Capability' Brown.

The temple itself is also worth a look; items paying homage to Shakespeare adorn its interior, including a replica bust of the playwright created by renowned sculptor Louis-François Roubiliac, the original of which is now housed in the British Museum. Other modern museum additions relating to Garrick himself are also on display and the Temple hosts a sweet summer programme of events appropriately including plays and music recitals.

BUSHY PARK

Teddington, TW11 0EQ
Opening times: 8am–10.30pm
Stations: Teddington, Hampton Wick, Hampton Court

Bushy Park—perched between Teddington and Hampton, Hampton Hill and Hampton Wick in the borough of Richmond-upon-Thames—is, according to the Royal Parks agency, "like a patchwork quilt of English History". As with the borough's eponymous parkland, Bushy was used extensively as deer hunting grounds for many years, specifically from when Henry VIII took over the three constituent swathes of land that make up the modern-day park from Cardinal Wolsey in 1529. But the grounds were and have been used for more idiosyncratic purposes; in the Medieval period, as well as for farming, the park was used for raising rabbits in man-made warrens, evidence of which can still be seen at the aptly named Warren Plantation and north of Lime and Chestnut Avenues.

During the First and Second World Wars the grounds of the park were used as the base for Canadian military forces—a totem pole was erected in the Woodland Garden in 1992 to notify this—and then the US Air Forces and Supreme Headquarters Allied Expeditionary Forces as Camp Griffiss, respectively. Subtle signs of the camps' existences survive in the stones and drain covers dotted around the grounds. The Upper Lodge Water Gardens—now fully restored after falling into disrepair with the culmination of their use in the development of Cold War defence technology—were utilised in both of these instances, but they now act as an impressive landscaped feature to the Park.

Charles I, in 1610, originally created the picturesque Longford River that runs through Bushy Park. Though a man-made channel, it now appears as a natural feature of the area's landscape and supports a variety of wildlife.

HAWTHORN
(CRATAEGUS MONOGYNA)
BERRIES HAVE LONG BEEN
USED TO MAKE JELLIES AND
JAMS, AND CONTROLLING
BLOOD PRESSURE

GUNNERSBURY NATURE TRIANGLE

Bollo Lane, Chiswick, W4 5LN
Opening times: 10am–4.30pm
Station: Chiswick Park

Over the years, the small, forested urban void located between the District tube and London Midland railway lines has developed into what is now known as the Gunnersbury Nature Triangle. An organic park with woodland, ponds, grassland, and even a swamp, the Triangle is home to a multitude of wildlife. Butterflies, birds and bats all populate the area, with the latter being especially significant; light pollution in the city has made it increasingly difficult for the creatures to find habitable environments, so the space is a welcome home for one of London's rarer residents.

Gunnersbury Nature Triangle constantly faces the unfortunate perils of inner-city life, and the threat of commercial development has loomed since the early 1980s. Friends of the triangle, the Chiswick Wildlife Group, vehemently opposed such plans, which lead to a public inquiry in 1983. The inquiry ruled in favour of the site remaining an urban natural habitat; a landmark result and the first time in UK legal history that an inquiry had done so. Despite the decision that it should remain a Local Nature Reserve—official classification came in 1987—the Triangle once again faces disruption by planned urban development, despite its being only one of 140 Sites of Metropolitan Importance.

CHISWICK HOUSE AND GARDENS

Burlington Lane, Chiswick, W4 2RP
Opening times: Sunday–Wednesday 10am–5pm, April–October
Station: Chiswick

The grand Palladian villa of Chiswick House which we see today was built in 1729 for the third Earl of Burlington as a locale to entertain guests and house his magnificent art collection. The building's gardens are more impressive than this conservative structure, having been an aesthetic inspiration for the nascent English Landscape Movement—notably in the expansive lawn gently sloping to the lake—as well as for the designs of both Blenheim Palace and New York's Central Park. These handsome grounds were the product of an overhaul in the early 1720s, transforming the existing geometric and formal Renaissance style layout—which suited the Jacobean building that existed prior to Chiswick House—into a more organic and natural landscape, with the sweeping lawns and artificial river still in situ.

Grandiose avenues and winding, interconnecting paths create opportunities for lengthy wandering. The grounds boast a grandiose variety of scenery, flora and fauna, as well as striking architectural accents such as the Renaissance-inspired cascade waterfall, Classical busts, the Inigo Jones-designed gateway, obelisk and Doric column. Thanks to a recent rejuvenation programme, the gardens can be enjoyed today almost exactly as they were in the early-eighteenth century.

HOLLAND PARK
KYOTO GARDEN

Holland Park Avenue, Notting Hill, W11 4UA
Opening times: 7.30am–dusk
Station: Holland Park

Holland Park is the largest green space in the Royal Borough of Kensington and Chelsea, encompassing an impressive 55.6 acres of land. Lying in the grounds of what was originally Cope Castle—the seventeenth century construction of Sir Walter Cope—the park offers facilities for sporting activities, as well as a large woodland that is ideal for wildlife watching.

Arguably the apex of the park's allure is the Japanese-style Kyoto Garden. Donated by the Chamber of Commerce of Kyoto as part of London's 1992 Japan Festival, the garden is set in an authentic design which offers the classic features of Japanese Gardening: stone lanterns, a waterfall, winding paths and a traditional *shishi-odoshi* ('deer scarer') water basin.

While most of the garden's immaculately manicured lawns are for viewing only, a more recent addition—the Fukushima Gardens, designed by Yasuo Kitayama and created in commemoration of the 2011 nuclear disaster—allow visitors an area to roam around, and interact with, more freely.

LONDON WETLAND CENTRE

Queen Elizabeth's Walk, Barnes, SW13 9WT
Opening times: 9.30am–6pm,
subject to change with seasons
Stations: Barnes, Barnes Bridge, Hammersmith

The WWT (Wildlife Wetlands Trust) London Wetland Centre, created in 2000, was voted the UK's favourite nature reserve in 2012 by *Countryfile Magazine*. Across its 105 acres there is an abundance of varied environments from lagoons, pools, and grazing marshes to wildflower meadows and reed beds, making the reservoir a serene site and a haven for a number of wildlife species.

There are dragonflies, butterflies, frogs, newts and water voles to spot, as well as the residents of Berkeley Bat House and the darling Asian short-clawed otters. Ornithologists will be particularly thrilled by the 200 plus species of bird that make their home in the wetlands—visible inconspicuously from one of the several hides placed throughout the park. The most impressive of these, the Peacock Tower, is a three-storey structure from which one can glean 360-degree views of the landscape. For less hands-on visitors, a heated observatory provides a comfortable means of watching the Centre's activity against the backdrop of London's cityscape.

As well as nature spotting and lengthy pathways, the Wetland Centre offers a variety of extra activities including free daily tours, wildlife photography courses and pond-dipping sessions, as well as two children's activity centres and a waterside café for a well-earned sit down.

MOUNT STREET GARDENS

South Audley Street, Mayfair, W1K 2TY
Station: Green Park

Located in a quiet residential backstreet in northern Mayfair, Mount Street Gardens is a quiet haven in the incessant bustle of central London. Originally established as a burial ground for the parish church of St George in Hanover Square in 1723, the formal function of the area was altered initially when an 1854 Act of Parliament was passed which disestablished central London burial grounds for health reasons, and further as the church's surrounding workhouses were relocated in 1871 due to overcrowding; the workhouse buildings were eventually demolished in 1886. Mount Street itself was widened and Carlos Place added, and the paths seen today were laid in 1889, completing the general layout of the gardens (excepting the bronze water fountain, now restored but originally designed by Sir Ernest George and Harold Peto in 1891).

Today, Mount Street Gardens' fauna comprises variously of London plane trees, an Australian silver wattle, three dawn redwoods, a Canary Island date palm, Chinese twisted willow and a ubiquitous common palm, as well as myriad shrubs and flowers. The Gardens also attract various species of bird, and budding ornithologists can make use of the installed bird identification chart.

BROMPTON CEMETERY

Fulham Road, SW10 9UG
Opening times: 8am–8pm Saturdays
Station: Fulham Broadway

Brompton Cemetery—designed by Benjamin Baud, who won a public competition with his concept for the site—opened its imposing gates in the early part of the nineteenth century, a time when the amount of burial space in the city was increasing vastly. Of the many aesthetically impressive examples built during this expansion, Brompton remains a significant example, lined with 27 Grade II memorials and a single Grade II* example in Burne-Jones' Leyland tomb.

Baud's design—both expensive and controversial for the time—borrows from several sources of Classical architecture in order to attain the atmosphere of a roofless cathedral; the chapel, inspired by St Peter's in Rome, is the centrepiece of the layout and functions as the altar, whilst the central avenue operates as the nave. Colonnades lead to the Grand Circle, in which the chapel is located, and under which sit the graveyard's catacombs, replete with their iconic, serpentile doors.

Brompton's graves act as totems to the city's eclectic history. Notable individuals who have been entombed at Brompton include: Emmeline Pankhurst, leader of the suffragette movement; Samuel Leigh Sotheby, antiquary and auctioneer; the shipping mogul Sir Samuel Cunard; and Long Wolf, a Native American performer with Buffalo Bill Cody's troop in the 1890s, who succumbed to Scarlet Fever while on tour at nearby Earl's Court. His monument—a tombstone adorned solely with the image of a lone wolf—stood for almost 100 years after his death, before his remains were disinterred and finally returned to his homeland.

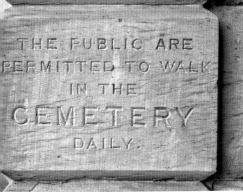

THE PUBLIC ARE
PERMITTED TO WALK
IN THE
CEMETERY
DAILY.

FULHAM PALACE GARDENS

Bishop's Avenue, SW6 6EA
Opening times: dawn–dusk, earlier closing times for the
Walled Garden subject to change with seasons
Station: Putney Bridge

Fulham Palace—now an open museum—was originally home to the various bishops of London. The bishop perhaps best known for enjoying the Palace's gardens was Henry Compton, who developed an extensive collection of plants during the seventeenth century; keenly interested in botany, he requested any reverends on mission around the world send back seeds, which led not only to a great collection of exotic tree specimens, but also to Compton's reputation as an influential character in botanical history.

Unfortunately Compton's successor, John Robinson, was less enthused by exoticism—preferring plants he could eat— and many beautiful specimens were removed or sold during his occupancy. Bishop Richard Terrick oversaw the landscaping of the gardens during the house's rebuilding in the 1760s, and what followed was a varied history as clergymen came and went.

The 1940s war effort meant that the garden couldn't receive adequate care and it fell into disrepair. Subsequent decades of regeneration have managed to recapture the charm—the Walled Garden being a particularly well-restored area. It is not all history, however; a new installation from Andrew Croft entitled *The Bishop's Tree* applies sculptures of some of the bishops and their animals to a cedar of Lebanon.

CHELSEA PHYSIC GARDEN

Royal Hospital Road, SW3 4HS
Opening times: 11am–6pm, April–October,
subject to change with seasons
Station: Sloane Square

Founded in 1673 by the Society of Apothecaries, the Chelsea Physic Garden is London's oldest botanic garden and houses a vast collection of over 5,000 plants. Included within its 100 species of trees are Britain's largest outdoor fruiting olive tree and the world's most northerly outdoor grapefruit tree. Due to its proximity to the Thames, the garden boasts a warm microclimate, which permits the nurturing of many uncommon or endangered plants as well as those otherwise unlikely to survive a British winter, such as the tropical and sub-tropical specimens housed in a series of glasshouses. The Grade II listed rock garden—built in 1773 with myriad exotic geological materials such as Icelandic lava and stones from the Tower of London—provides an additional habitat for a distinctive array of exotic plant life.

The Garden's original purpose—to provide a source for education in the identification of plants and their uses—has shaped its long history, and a series of themed gardens, displaying global ethnic and indigenous applications of plants in food and medicine continue to promote such knowledge. An international seed exchange programme, instigated in the 1700s by the Chelsea Physic Garden and Leidon University, continues to this day, enabling botanic gardens from around the world—there are currently participants in over 30 countries—to cultivate foreign specimens.

YORK HOUSE GARDENS

Sion Road, Twickenham, TW1 3DD
Opening times: dawn–dusk
Station: Twickenham

York House, a seventeenth century stately home situated in Twickenham, was originally built for Andrew Pitcarne, courtier to King Charles I. Following Pitcarne's death, a mere decade after its construction, York House spent centuries changing hands amongst aristocrats, artists, ambassadors and politicians.

Sir Ratan Tata, a Parsi industrialist and businessman involved in the trade of steel and opium—and York House's owner at the beginning of the twentieth century—was renowned for entertaining in the house and made a lasting tangible impression on its grounds with this in mind. Though he passed away in 1918, leaving the house to be purchased by Twickenham council in 1926, its gardens still bear his touch.

In addition to a stunning sunken lawn, statues of sea nymphs sculpted by Oscar Spalmach and imported from Rome feature throughout the gardens. *The Oceanides* are a stunningly dramatic collection of nudes in pearl white Carrara marble, which create a sense of theatre amongst the modern day civic offices—a spectacular depiction of Venus, Roman goddess of love, forms an impressive centrepiece.

For those of a more bashful disposition, there is still plenty on offer; a restored Japanese garden allows for a quieter experience, and the council has provided tennis courts for public use.

RICHMOND PARK

Between Richmond, Kingston, Ham, and Sheen
Opening times: 7am/7.30am (summer/winter)–dusk
Station: Richmond

Richmond Park is the largest and perhaps the best loved of London's Royal Parks, and its bucolic expanse of lakes, grassland, undulating hills, lodges, ancient woodland and rich variety of wildlife has been officially designated a Site of Special Scientific Interest and a National Nature Reserve.

Hunting and the monarchy have been synonymous with the Park's history. Fleeing to Richmond Palace to escape the plague in 1625, Charles I introduced 2,000 deer to the area and subsequently, in 1637, enclosed the land with an eight mile-long wall—portions of which still stand, albeit in a restored form— much to the consternation of the local landowners and farmers who had legitimate claims to the land. Such was the furore that the king was forced to reinstate public entry to the park, as well as building a ladder in to the wall for locals to access and collect firewood.

The following centuries saw further developments made, including the creation of watering ponds, the planting of new woodland— including the charming ornamental Isabella Plantation—and the planning of two vistas. Of these, the protected view from King Henry's Mound in the west of the Park to a distant St Paul's remains one of the hidden highlights, now replete with a functioning telescope and a set of ornately sculpted tercentenary gates.

Nearby, in Poet's Corner, is another idiosyncratic detail of the Park. The contemporary Ian Dury bench—a memorial to the Blockheads frontman—at first appears inconspicuous, though a closer look reveals the inscription "REASONS TO BE CHEERFUL", and a solar-powered headphone port loaded with eight different musical pieces by the late singer.

ACKNOWLEDGEMENTS

Many thanks to Amy Cooper-Wright, Leonardo Collina and Paul Cavanagh for their elegant and thoughtful design on the book; to Leanne Hayman for her indispensable editorial work throughout the project; and to Conni Rosewarne, Phoebe Adler, Patrick Q Fisher, John Hewish, Marc Nuckballs and Richard Duffy for their extensive research, writing and proofing assistance.

Thanks to all of the individuals and societies who provided imagery and information for the book's profiles—especially Gia Houck and Stephanie Wolff—without all of whom the publication would not have been possible.

IMAGE CREDITS

cover, copyright (clockwise from top left): Lewis Mitchell; Stephanie Wolff; Leonardo Collina; Friends of King Henrys Walk Garden.

pp. 2–3, 18–25, 32–33, 38–41, 114–115, 118–119, 122–123, 128–131, 132–133, 136–137, 142–145, 148–151, 168–169, 170–171, 186, 187 bottom: Photography by Leonardo Collina

pp. 4, 78 top and bottom right: Courtesy Rachel Pfleger and Dan Neal.

pp. 9, 28–31, 44–45, 52–55, 58–59, 61 top and bottom left, 62–63, 74–75, 182–183: Copyright Stephanie Wolff

pp. 26–27, 189 top: Photography by Thomas Howells

pp. 36–37, 42–43, 102–103, 146–147, 176–177, 184–185: Photography by Frederick Williams

pp. 48–51, 56–57, 60, 70–71, 78 bottom left, 79, 90–93, 98–99: Photography by Amy Cooper-Wright

pp. 164 top, 184, 185 top: Courtesy Historic Royal Palaces

pp. 12–13: Courtesy Friends of St George's Gardens

p. 16: Photography by Clive Darra

p. 17: Copyright Lee Mawdsley

pp. 34–35: Courtesy Spitalfields City Farm

pp. 64, 65 top left and bottom left: Courtesy The Friends of Parkland Walk

p. 65 right: Photography by Jelm6

p. 66 top: Courtesy David Holt

p. 66 bottom: Courtesy Christian Heilman

pp. 67, 68–69: Courtesy Laura Delnevo

pp. 72–73: Photography by Brett Jordan

p. 76: Photography by MongFish

p. 77: Courtesy Abney Park Trust

pp. 80–83: Courtesy Friends of King Henrys Walk Garden

pp. 88–89: Courtesy Hackney City Farm

pp. 94–95: Photography by Daren Clarke

pp. 96–97: Courtesy Matthew Black

pp. 100–101: Courtesy Mudchute City Farm

p. 104: Courtesy The Geffrye Museum, Photography by Sunniva Harte

pp. 105 top: Courtesy of The Geffrye Museum, Photography by Richard Davies; bottom left; Courtesy of The Geffrye Museum, Photography by

Mandy Williams; bottom right; Courtesy of The Geffrye Museum, Photography by Sunniva Harte

pp. 84–85, 106–107: Courtesy Surrey Docks Farm

p. 110: Courtesy Peter Staniforth

pp. 111 bottom left and top, 112–113: Photography by Dave Taskis

p. 111 bottom right: Photography by Alan Chown

p. 122 top: Courtesy Claire Woollam

p. 122 bottom: Tom Page

p. 123: Courtesy Robert Cutts

p. 124 bottom: Photography by Garry Knight

pp. 124 top, 125, 126–127: Photography by Herry Lawford

pp. 138–139: Courtesy English Heritage

pp. 140–141: Courtesy Vauxhall City Farm

pp. 140–141: Courtesy Bankside Open Spaces Trust

pp. 152–153, 154–155, 166–167: Photography by Markham Cole

pp. 156–157: Photography by David Loftus

pp. 158–159: Photography by Keiko Oikawa

pp. 160–161: Photography by Maxwell Hamilton

p. 162 top: Courtesy Historic Royal Palaces

p. 162 bottom: Photography by Chris Capstick

p. 163 top and centre: Courtesy Richard Lea-Hair/ Historic Royal Palaces/ newsteam.co.uk; bottom: Courtesy Andrea Jones/ Historic Royal Palaces/ newsteam.co.uk

pp. 164–165: Photography by Carole King

pp. 172–173: Courtesy The Royal Borough of Kensington and Chelsea

p. 174: Photography by Ross Paxton

p. 175 bottom: Photography by David Howarth; top right: Photography by Richard Taylor Jones; top left: Photography by Jamie Wyver

pp. 178, 179 bottom left and top: Photography by Gia Houck

p. 179 bottom right: Photography by Mike Steele

pp. 180, 181 bottom: Courtesy Robin Forster/ Historic Royal Palaces

p. 181 top: Photography by Andrew Frost

pp. 188–189: Copyright Lewis Mitchell

Black Dog Publishing Limited
10A Acton Street
London
WC1X 9NG

t.   44 (0)207 713 5097
f.   44 (0)207 713 8682
e.   info@blackdogonline.com
w.   www.blackdogonline.com

Edited by Leanne Hayman and Thomas Howells.
Designed at Black Dog Publishing by Amy Cooper-Wright
and Leonardo Collina.

ISBN 978 1 907317 96 5

Black Dog Publishing is an environmentally responsible company.
London Out of Sight is printed on sustainably sourced paper.

art design fashion
history photography
theory and things

www.blackdogonline.com